Sea Hill Press, Inc.
P.O. Box 60301
Santa Barbara, CA 93160
www.seahillpress.com

ISBN: 978-1-937720-14-8

Printed in Hong Kong

THE VOICES OF STONES

This book is dedicated to all those who have allowed me into their lives at their darkest hours. You have granted me a rare privilege that I will always cherish, honor, and protect. In sharing your journey through loss, pain, and recovery you have given me, and so many others, hope and renewal.

Thank you from the depths of my heart.

Acknowledgments

I am grateful to many for making The Wisdom of Stones such a success and for helping me create The Voices of Stones. First, I want to thank my publisher, Greg Sharp, President of Sea Hill Press, for his support and encouragement. He gives me enough support to make this process fun and enough direction to create a quality outcome.

The people of Campobello Island continue to be supportive and encouraging. The island, its history, and the testimony of its people's lives, speak to the harsh realities of loss and the victory of hope. Their lives and the stories my writing and photographs have prompted them to share continue to profoundly influence my life and work.

My friend Cliff Culp once again assisted greatly in the technical portions of these images. Our friendship grows despite his frustration with my limited technical skills.

Donna played a major role in the initial capture of many of these images. Her eye is remarkable and her help invaluable. I especially appreciate her willingness to endure shooting at night at the edge of the Bay of Fundy's incoming tide.

My grandson, Matthew, continues to be a joy in all parts of my life. When he is present on Campobello, I always see this island and its stones with fresh eyes.

Introduction

THE RESPONSE TO THE WISDOM OF STONES HAS BEEN GRATIFYING BEYOND DESCRIPTION. I HAVE BEEN MOVED BY THE VERY PERSONAL AND POWERFUL STORIES THE BOOK HAS ALLOWED PEOPLE TO SHARE WITH ME. I AM VERY GRATEFUL AND HUMBLED.

MY DESIRE TO CREATE THE VOICES OF STONES IS THE PRODUCT OF MANY INFLUENCES IN MY LIFE; PERHAPS SOME OF WHICH I AM STILL UNAWARE. ONE PART OF MY LIFE THAT HEAVILY INFLUENCED THIS EFFORT (AND MANY OTHER PARTS OF MY LIFE) IS MY WORK OVER SEVERAL DECADES AS A PSYCHOLOGIST FOCUSING ON LARGE SCALE TRAUMAS SUCH AS DISASTER AND TERRORISM. I SOMETIMES TELL PEOPLE THAT MY CAREER CONSISTED OF GOING TO THE NICEST PLACES AT THE WORST POSSIBLE TIMES.

IT MAY SOUND STRANGE TO SOME, BUT FOR ME, IT HAS BEEN A GREAT HONOR AND PRIVILEGE TO BE WITH INDIVIDUALS, FAMILIES, AND COMMUNITIES IN THEIR DARKEST HOURS. AND THEY WERE INDEED DARK HOURS. I WITNESSED THE TERRIBLE AFTERMATH OF TORNADOES, FLOODS, FIRES, EARTHQUAKES AND HURRICANES.

I WAS IN NEW YORK CITY LESS THAN TWO DAYS FOLLOWING 9/11 AND PRESENT IN OKLAHOMA CITY AND NAIROBI, KENYA, SHORTLY AFTER TERRORIST BOMBINGS THERE. ONE OF MY MOST DIFFICULT DAYS WAS ACCOMPANYING THEN VICE PRESIDENT AND MRS. GORE TO MEET WITH THE FAMILIES OF THOSE KILLED IN THE SCHOOL SHOOTINGS IN LITTLETON, COLORADO.

n the course of these powerful experiences, I learned a great deal about how we respond to, and continue life after, such devastating events. Two factors always walk alongside victims and survivors as they move forward with their lives.

First is loss. All of these events involve loss of some type. The type, such as life, home, job, friends, and magnitude vary significantly...but there is always loss. Loss is part of life. It varies only by type, time, and how we respond.

Second, hope is a major factor in how people continue in their lives. Do we lose hope? Can we maintain or regain hope? I have witnessed the power of hope in what often seems like hopeless situations. How we understand and manage loss and maintain hope is a defining challenge for all of us.

Can we place the loss in the context of our life's course as well as personal, family, and community history? Can we find perspective in understanding the experience as it compares to other losses and tragedies

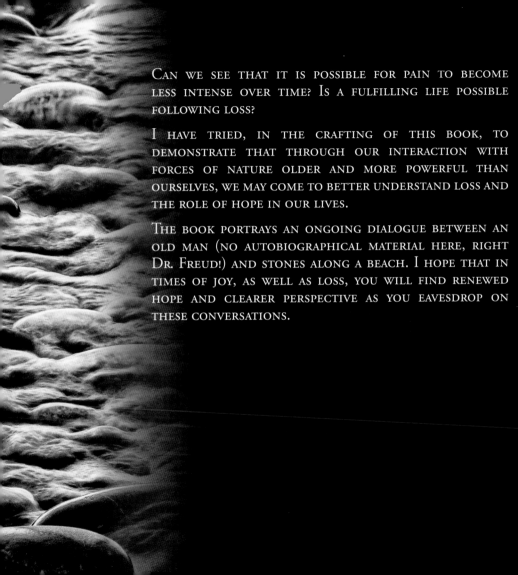

Can we see that it is possible for pain to become less intense over time? Is a fulfilling life possible following loss?

I have tried, in the crafting of this book, to demonstrate that through our interaction with forces of nature older and more powerful than ourselves, we may come to better understand loss and the role of hope in our lives.

The book portrays an ongoing dialogue between an old man (no autobiographical material here, right Dr. Freud!) and stones along a beach. I hope that in times of joy, as well as loss, you will find renewed hope and clearer perspective as you eavesdrop on these conversations.

THE AGREEMENT

The sun began to ark higher off the horizon and the snows had turned again to water. On the first warm day, the old man returned once more to walk the rocky shoreline.

He had missed the touch and sound of the stones beneath his feet. He had missed the sounds the stones made when they roll in the gentle surf. It was like meeting an old friend again after a long absence. As he walked, he once again felt the connection grow.

He walked until after the sun vanished and moonlight illuminated the stones. As he walked, his heart gave voice to the question he had waited all winter to ask.

And the old man said, "Stones, will you speak to me, and with your voice share with me your wisdom?"

And the stones said, "Why should we speak to you?"

The old man replied, "Because we are both old, but you are far older and wiser than I."

And the stones said, "Why have you selected us? Surely there are those as old and perhaps even wiser."

And the old man said, "Because, in my soul, I know that your voice has been heard by my forefathers in the ancient days. They lived in Ireland, a rocky island much like this one.

You spoke to them while they worked her fields. You spoke to them while they walked her rocky coast. You spoke to them as they struggled to survive. You spoke to them as they left Ireland to make new lives. So, in that long line of my ancestors, I have come once again to seek and hear your voices of wisdom."

And the stones said, "Of what will we speak old man?"

He replied, "As my days on earth become fewer, I need even more than before to have you speak to me of loss and hope. I have far too much of the first and far too little of the latter. Help me understand the meeting of the stones, water, and sky. Speak to me of why I feel so alone? Help me understand why I am here and how to have hope as I live out my days."

The stones remained silent. Then, in the turning of four tides, they spoke again to the old man. The stones said, "You must agree to three conditions if we are to speak with you."

And the old man said, "Please, tell me what I must do."

The stones said, "First, you must agree to be silent and listen while we speak."

The old man said with a faint smile, "While that is not the natural way of men with Irish blood, I will be silent."

"Second, you must agree to walk slowly among us and not hurry."

"That is easy," he replied. "Moving slowly is what old men do best."

The stones said, "Finally, you must agree to take what we tell you and live out your days in harmony with what you have been told, and you must share this knowledge with others. We cannot spend our time talking to everybody. That is only one of our jobs."

The old man replied, "Ah, this is the hardest thing you have asked. I cannot promise to be successful. But, I will promise to do my very best. I promise to honor you and your wisdom, and in so doing, I honor my forefathers. I will help guide those who still will listen to the words of an old man."

The stones paused. They rolled against each other as a small wave washed over them. Then they said, "We have a bargain. We will speak to you, and in our voices you will know the wisdom of the stones."

"Tell me," said the old man,
"why do so many of us wish to hear your voice
and share your wisdom?"

And the stones answered...

We are the gateway to the sea
from where all things come.

We are the entrance to the land
and your first guide.

We are the place

where all life takes root and grows.

We are where all life
and all dreams take flight.

We are your protectors
when the sea grows harsh.

I am the stone at water's edge.

I stand at the edge of the place
from which you came.

I stand at the edge of where you live.

I stand at the place
to which your heart will always return.

We are the edge.

We are the point where land, sky, and water touch. This is where your past and your future touch. This is the place where grief dies. This is the place where hope is born anew. Right here. Right now.

And the old man said,

"How am I to understand loss?

It is everywhere...

Each day it grows more heavy on my heart."

And the stones answered...

First we must understand circles and spheres.

We must understand that there is
no beginning,
no end,
only where we join
and where we leave.

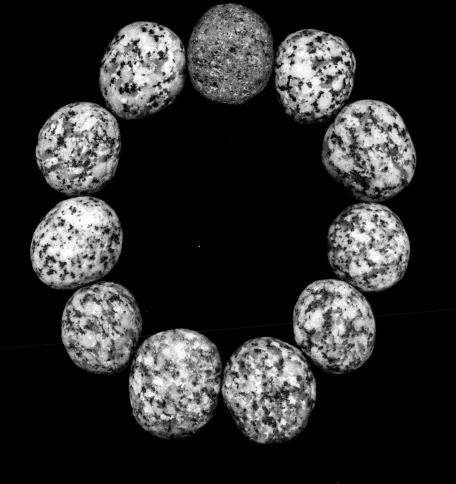

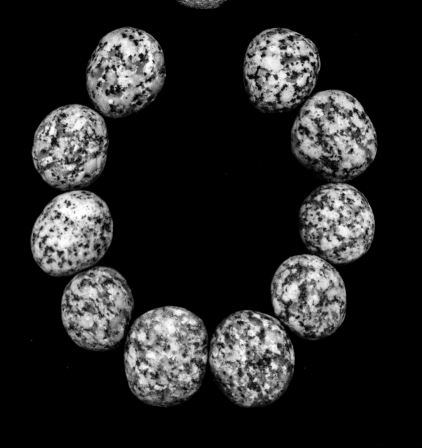

That which is lost is not gone.

It only exists apart from us.

Look inside to find what is lost and hold it within.

In loss, we feel we are different,
separated from everything. Alone.

We are not.

We stand in the presence
of all who have gone before us.
Like us, they have all known loss...
but we continue.

It is a fine line that marks the difference between
joy and pain,
losing and finding,
living and dying.

In times of great loss it feels like our pain creates gaps in our souls that are too wide to ever span.

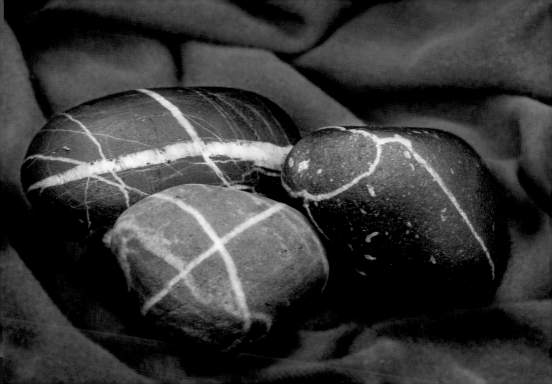

As we struggle, it feels like we have been split in every direction and nothing makes sense.

Sometimes the depth of our loss feels like it has damaged us to the core of our very being; that it has changed who we are.

Who among us has not known loss and damage?
Each of us has been, or will be, separated from
that which makes us whole.

We are the ones who get hurt
when we try to hold too tight
to that which is not ready to be held tightly.

Grief is the dividend of our investment in others.

Without investment there is no loss.

Without loss there is no grief.

We earn our grief with our investment in others.

It is therefore a precious dividend not to be

shunned, but to be embraced.

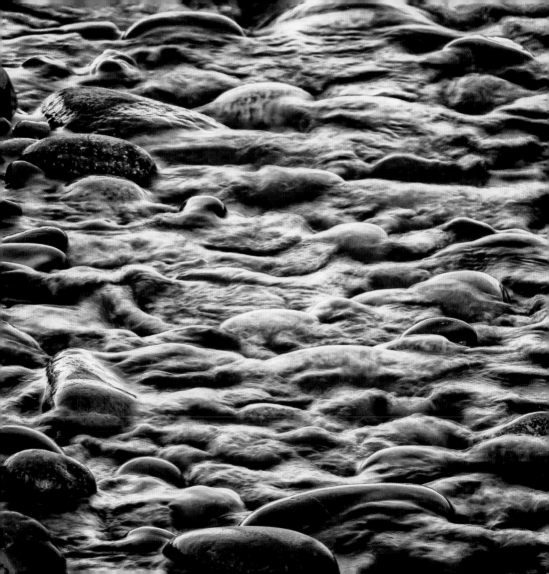

And the old man said,

"But how can I go on? Where can I find hope at

the other side of loss?"

Give your tears to the stones.

We will hold your pain.

The fog of loss will burn away
as hope shines brighter.

In the fog of loss, remember that just because you cannot see something does not mean it is not there.

There will always be something to guide us.

Sometimes we must look hard.

There is comfort
in gathering with others and being held by those
who have themselves been broken.

They understand us.

There are those who seem destined
to hold those who are fragile.

we are often surprised to find ourselves held and

protected by those who are so unlike us.

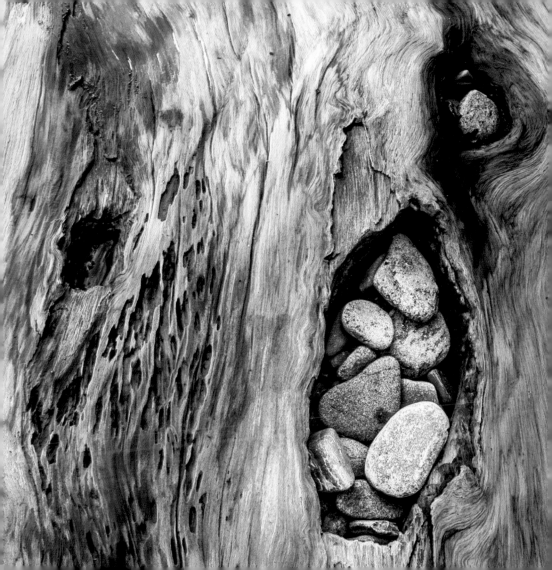

If we take time to look deep into the world around us, we will come to know ourselves better.

Be patient with yourself.

You are the only person who will be with you for all of your life.

Do not despair even if the wise point you in different directions.

There are many paths through loss.

enter back into the world slowly and gently.

...except if you decide to come back

in a different way!

And the old man said,

"Your voice has been wise and clear. You have

helped me understand loss, and I leave you with

hope in my heart. I thank you for indulging an old

man." He hesitated as he turned to go, and asked,

"In the tradition of my ancestors, will you speak to

me a blessing before we part?"

And the stones replied...

May loving hands hold you gently and protect you.

May the tides of the world cleanse you
and be gentle as they guide you.

And may you understand

the wishing Stone's wish:

wish upon me wisely.

Let your wishes not be frivolous.

Let your wishes be for others.

And understand that you make

your own wishes come true.

Brian Flynn is a psychologist by training and formerly served as a Rear Admiral/Assistant Surgeon General in the U.S. Public Health Service. He is currently an Associate Director of the Center for the Study of Traumatic Stress, in the Department of Psychiatry, at the Uniformed Services University of the Health Sciences, Bethesda, Maryland.

His work has been focused primarily on large-scale trauma—disasters and terrorism. He credits these experiences with fueling his passion to find beauty where others do not (or cannot), to find order in what others see as randomness and chaos, and to nurture hope and meaning where and when he can.

He is an accomplished photographer. His photos have won numerous awards. He and his wife, Donna, live near Annapolis, Maryland, and on Campobello Island, New Brunswick, Canada.

Photograph by Donna Flynn